I Believe

DYLIN BELLIS

ISBN-13: 978-1-953300-21-8
eISBN-13: 978-1-953300-22-5

Sales: Most Clay Bridges titles are available in special quantity discounts.
Custom imprinting or excerpting can also be done to fit special needs. Contact
Clay Bridges at Info@ClayBridgesPress.com.

For my family and friends, thank you for always believing in me.

Contents

Whoa Moment

Full circle moments are pretty cool. They make us stop, reflect, and astonish at the goodness that God has to offer.

A full-circle moment inspired this book. I was sitting on my bed, straight out of the shower. I had just finished reading my devotions and I began to pray, just as I usually do every night. Towards the end of my prayer, I said, "Whoa. Lord, I believe in YOU."

In this moment, I realized that every experience leading up to this point in my life had a purpose. Every experience was God's way of not only leading me to Him, but it was also His way of leading me to fully believe in His goodness and faithfulness.

I have reached a place where I am thankful for every tough situation that I have gone through because, without those experiences, I would not have the relationship with Christ that I have.

I want to share all of these experiences with the world because God's goodness is far too good to keep hidden. I want to share them with you because you might be experiencing something similar. You might be in a place and have no idea what the purpose of that place is.

I have grown to learn that every place and season has a purpose. Everything you experience will eventually work itself out and make sense. I had my *whoa* moment, and it inspired me to share with you the journey that led me to it.

My hope and prayer is that whatever you are experiencing will strengthen you, guide you, and help you grow into a better version of yourself. I hope that one day you will be able to have a *whoa* moment and that you will be able to be grateful for everything that you have experienced.

Falling Apart

I always had a plan. My twin sister, Delaney, and I have always been different. I am uptight and organized, and Delaney is unbothered and laid back.

When we entered high school, we started making plans for our lives after graduation. Because I have a passion for writing, I planned my future based on that. At the beginning of my sophomore year, my plan was to attend Susquehanna University to major in English: Publishing and Editing.

I had it figured out, and my sister did not. When someone asked her what she planned to do after high school, she would respond, "I have no clue." *What in the world was wrong with her? How could she not have any ideas?* For a while, I was concerned for her. It baffled me that someone could be so nonchalant about a big decision.

Fast forward to the end of our sophomore year. Delaney had a "plan." She discovered an interest in biology and was excited about finally having an idea. Not only was I happy for her, but my whole family was also happy for her. Delaney finally had a plan, and mine was slowly starting to fade away.

God had spoken to me on multiple occasions about ministry, but I pretended that I did not hear Him. No matter how hard I tried, God kept speaking to me when I least expected Him to.

I vividly remember one occasion in particular. I was walking home from school, following the same route that I had taken routinely. The road that I frequently travel happens to pass by my church's parsonage. As I passed the property, God called me to ministry and reminded me of His plan. I naturally tried to ignore Him, but I could not get the thought out of my head.

I was reminded of this exact moment a few nights ago when a Bible verse popped up on my phone.

Revelation 3:20 (NIV)
"Here I am! I stand at the door and knock. If anyone hears my voice and opens the door, I will come in and eat with that person, and they with me."

I kept the door closed on God by ignoring His knock. Despite my unwillingness to listen, He kept knocking, just as He had promised.

For quite some time, I thought that I had complete authority over my future. I learned the hard way that my future is not in my hands, but completely in God's. It took a lot of disappointment, hard conversations, and harsh realizations to comprehend this reality.

After spending five days in North Carolina on a mission trip with my youth group, the plan that I had previously formed completely unraveled. I felt restless and unsettled in the weeks leading up to the trip. I prayed and asked God to give me a sign.

A sign for what? I have no idea what I was asking God to give me, but I knew that I wanted Him to speak to me in some way during the trip.

When God did not immediately give me the sign that I was asking for, I became impatient. *Come on God, I'm only going to be here for two more days.* Thoughts like this circled through my head as the days passed.

The last day of the trip arrived and God *finally* gave me a sign. Pastor Ryan, the pastor at our host church, asked me what my plans were after high school. I immediately replied, "I'm not really sure." I have no idea why I responded this way because I thought I had a plan. He proceeded to ask me if college was an option. Again, I responded, "I'm not really sure." Pastor Ryan looked at me and said, "I believe the church is changing."

When I went on that trip, I was a completely different person than I am now. The person that attended that trip interpreted his words as, "I don't need to go to college." I was so excited that God gave me a sign that I didn't stop to think, "Is that really what his words meant?" Thank goodness I have learned the art of discernment since this moment.

Looking back, I realize that Pastor Ryan meant exactly what he said. The church is changing. He did not say throw all caution to the wind and *very* firmly decide not to attend college. I thought that God had given me my next step, but in reality, He did nothing more than open a door for me. A door that would eventually lead to growth, obedience, and peace.

When I returned from my trip to North Carolina, I knew I needed to tell my parents about my new "plan." I put it off for a few days until one night, I just blurted it out. I was sitting at the head of our kitchen table, and working on my computer. My mom was standing at the sink, and my dad was standing in front of the refrigerator. It's odd how vividly I remember this moment.

Out of nowhere, I said, "I don't think I'm going to college." I will never forget the look on my mom's face. She slowly turned her head, looked at me, and hardly said anything. My dad was surprisingly calm and reminded me that he would always support me in whatever I chose to do. He didn't exactly do cartwheels through the kitchen. To say that I shocked them would be an understatement.

The same exact thing happened when I told my grandparents. My Mimi's jaw almost touched the floor. My Pa would not stop asking me how I planned to make a living. My Nana asked me question after question after question. My Pappy, who is a pretty quiet guy, stayed true to himself and did not say much.

My family's reactions should have alerted me. Not a single person seemed thrilled or confident about my decision. Quite honestly, neither was I. I thought that I was following God's plan for my life, but I was doing the complete opposite. Instead of feeling at peace and filled with joy, I was confused and unhappy.

I started to resent my sister for having a "plan," and I understood the feelings and thoughts that she had for years. In the following weeks, I walked on eggshells around my mom because we could not have a conversation without the subject coming up. I cried when I prayed at night and read my devotions. I found myself withdrawing from family members who I used to share everything with.

The outcome that hurt me the most was that I found myself straying away from God. I would pray and would not feel peace. I would read my Bible, but I could not seem to trust the words that I was reading. The only word to accurately describe me was lost.

I'm pretty good at hiding my feelings in front of people. Because of my personality, I do not like to place myself in a vulnerable position. The thought of being an open book about everything does not sit well with me. (Writing this book was very intimidating and scary.)

One night at youth group, we were having a group discussion. The members of my small group were all girls and people that I knew I could trust. We each went around in a circle and answered a question. When it came time for me to give my response, I could barely get through my answer without crying. I can't even tell you what the topic was, or if my answer even related to the topic.

I hate crying in front of people because if there would ever be a contest for the world's ugliest crier, I would definitely be entered. As tears rolled down my cheeks, my friends offered encouragement and I managed to pull myself together on the outside. On the inside, I was as far from together that a person can get.

After the lesson, Sydney, one of my closest friends, pulled me aside, and asked if I needed a hug. I completely lost it.

Alicia, my youth group leader and one of my biggest role models, pulled me aside, sat down on a couch with me, and asked me what was going on. I told her everything, and I'm so glad I did. She reassured me that none of us are supposed to know God's plan completely.

Michelle, my friend Alana's mom, and another role model of mine prayed with me and offered support.

One of my biggest takeaways from this night is that having a community is extremely important. For me, my community includes my Christian friends and supporters who will encourage me, support me, give me wise advice, and pick me up when I fall down.

Although I have plenty of friends who are not related to me by blood, I was also born with an already established community. I am one of the lucky 40 million people in the world who was born with a twin.

I get asked often if I enjoy being a twin. I can't really answer that because I don't know what it is like to not be one. My normal is always having to share my stuff, always having a person to bicker with, and always having a friend.

Sometimes, I will admit, I do wish I had some extended alone time. For instance, my twin sister and I go everywhere together. We go to soccer practice, my grandparents' house, the grocery store, and even work together. Driving a car by myself is a VERY rare occurrence. I look forward to every time I work by myself or have a doctor's appointment because I know that I will have alone time in the car. I use these rare opportunities to spend some quiet time with God and myself.

Although I yearn for alone time, I would never change the way my life is. I love having a built-in best friend. My sister is my closest friend and supporter. Whenever I need advice, she's the first person I turn to. I love having her as a part of my community.

I also understand that everyone is not as fortunate as I am when it comes to having a community, and that's okay. God has provided other Christians for us each to have one. Let's not forget that we will always have someone to turn to because God will always be there for us. He does not want us to remain alone.

When we lack community, we lack accountability. My favorite thing about my sister is if she sees me doing something that isn't the best idea, she'll tell me and save me from a bad decision or an awkward situation. She doesn't just tell me what I want to hear. She tells me her honest opinion, even if I won't like what she has to say.

If you have found your community, I'm so happy for you. Keep those friends close and rely on each other. Don't forget to always be the friend that someone was for you. Sometimes those strong people in your community need you more than you need them.

If you do not have a support system or people that genuinely care about your well being, take a good look at the people around you. You probably have more of a community than what you think, and you're probably just too stubborn to ask for help.

I didn't walk away from the couch that night completely at peace. I eventually rebuilt my relationship with Christ, made peace with my mom, and realized that I was in a season of waiting. I was incredibly impatient, but I quickly learned the importance of growth during that time.

According to Proverbs 16:9 (NIV)), "In their hearts humans plan their course, but the Lord establishes their steps." I was trying to plan my course. Throughout the entire process of deciding not to attend college, I realized that I didn't talk to God. I wasn't lost because I didn't have a clear path. I was lost because along the way, I lost sight of God. Because I refocused my attention on Him, and the plan that He had for my life, I can confidently say that I believe in His plan now more than I ever have.

I finally opened the door for God and responded to His knocking. When I did, His promise held true: He was there waiting for me. He had never left my side and He continues to walk alongside me.

I have also discovered that God cares about your dreams and plans.

---

1 John 5:14 (NIV)
"This is the confidence we have in approaching God: that if we ask anything according to his will, he hears us."

Our plans and dreams might not come into fruition, but that's okay because God's plan will always be better. We can be sure that God will hear our requests.

Although I had to go through some rough experiences to reach this point in my walk with Christ, I am grateful for everything that I have experienced.

My devotional tonight assigned me the task of writing ten things that I am grateful for. One of the items that I listed was hard times because it was during this hard time that I grew as a person and as a Christian.

[1]If you feel lost and confused, start by refocusing yourself on God. If you've lost your relationship with Christ, get it back. He is waiting for you with open arms. Have a little bit of faith and trust in God's plan because He ultimately determines our steps, despite our efforts to plan our own course.

---

[1] Live in Light: 5-minute devotions for teen girls
Melanie Redd
Emeryville, California
2019
Althea Press
Pg. 133

Get Real

My prayers have transformed a LOT over the last year. The transformation began one night when my frustration outweighed my joy. I was sitting on my bed, reading my devotions, and it was right around the time that I started questioning God BIG time. I would pray and ask God for answers, and His only response was to be still and relax in His presence. He kept reminding me to enjoy the season that I was currently in.

I can be pretty impatient, so you can imagine that this did not sit well with me. I kept hiding my frustration and anger from God, repeatedly acting like He did not already know that I was experiencing these things. In case you forgot, He knows everything, so this was a pretty foolish move on my part.

Ironically, the devotional I read that night was focused around telling God exactly how you feel. Taking those words to heart, I prayed very openly that night. I completely opened my heart and mind to God and let it ALL out.

I specifically remember saying out loud, "God, I am angry at you." I half-expected myself to feel guilty for being mad at God. The reality of the situation was the exact opposite. God simply responded, "It's okay."

I just told God that I was angry with Him, and the only thing that He had to say was "okay." You might think that I'm crazy, that I have totally lost my mind. I'll admit that I thought the same thing at that moment. Now, I feel nothing but gratitude.

That moment completely changed my relationship with Christ. Instead of feeling guilty for being angry with God, I felt peace and relief. The frustration that I had kept inside for several weeks was let out, and the anger that I had felt was taken away. God not only told me that it was okay, but He also comforted me. My relationship with Him grew immensely, and I am forever grateful for that devotional that inspired me to get real with God.

God already knows everything that you're thinking and feeling, so instead of hiding your thoughts and feelings, share them with Him.

Outside appearances are incredibly deceiving, and it can be easy to put on a fabricated appearance. As a lover of books, I am very familiar with the phrase, "Don't judge a book by its cover." Sometimes a book that looks like it would appeal to me does not. Other times, a book looks terrible and I really enjoy it.

For a moment, let's pretend there's a middle-aged woman that lives in the apartment next to you. Every day, you pass her in the lobby on your way to work. She greets you with a warm smile and a friendly hello. Day after day, she carries a steaming travel mug of coffee as she exits through the double doors.

Your middle-aged neighbor appears to be living an ideal life. In reality, she's not happy working in the corporate building down the street. She can barely pay for her groceries, gas, and rent. On top of that, her boyfriend just broke up with her one week before Valentine's Day.

I know the last part, more like the whole part, sounds like the plot of a Hallmark movie, but try to keep your attention focused on the difference between her outward appearance and her inner turmoil. On the outside, your neighbor looks like she is full of light. On the inside, she is experiencing sadness and darkness. Once again, we see that outward appearances are incredibly misleading.

Our circumstances present themselves in the opposite way. On the outside, they appear to be filled with darkness. On the inside, they are actually filled with some light. The problem is that we're so focused on the darkness that we forget to look for the light.

John 8: 12 (NIV)
"Again Jesus spoke to them, saying, 'I am the light of the world. Whoever follows me will not walk in darkness, but will have the light of life.'"

The verse above does not say that you will always see Jesus' light. It also doesn't say that He only shines His light on Tuesdays and Thursdays. It tells us that if we follow Him, we will not walk in darkness.

If you're having trouble seeing His light, take a look at yourself. When is the last time you read your Bible? When was the last time you spoke to God?

Your inability to see God's light is a result of you unintentionally taking your attention off of His light. If you're a follower of Jesus, if you believe in Him, He promises us that you will not walk in darkness. He promises us that His light will not be hidden. So if you're struggling to see God's light, you've covered up His light with the darkness of your situation. You have placed more focus on the darkness than His light.

This past year, I placed my focus on the darkness around me. I had covered up God's light and decided to find it again. Acknowledging that you have placed your focus on the darkness around you and not doing anything about it is like going into the grocery store with a list and coming out with nothing.

Make a change, and find God's light again. More importantly, let it shine. Allow it to brighten those dark areas in your life.

Necessary Wilderness

When I was growing up in my church, we learned about Jesus' time in the wilderness during Sunday school. Each time I would hear this story, I would picture Jesus in the middle of a vast area that contained lots of sand and dirt. I also pictured an area that contained few people, animals, and water.

One night, I was doing my devotions and I came across the story of Jesus in the wilderness. It had been a long time since I actually read the story. It amazed me that despite temptation and privation, Jesus continued to turn to God. Reading the scripture reminded me that we all require a wilderness.

I felt really deflated and lost for several weeks the summer before my junior year of high school because God was not responding to my prayers in the same way that He had in the past. Up until this point, I would ask God for an answer and He would respond relatively quickly.

This time was completely different. I asked God what I should be doing and He did not respond immediately. He also did not respond with a clear answer. He simply told me to "be still." *What does that mean?*

For about a year, I had a "project" to work on. Whether it was writing a book or preparing for my faith night, I had something to pour my energy into. I got into a routine of diligently working on something every day. Even if I was not directly working on something, my mind was always coming up with new ideas and planning every detail.

When God told me to "be still," I did not know how to respond. My mind hardly ever shut off, and I always felt like I should be planning something. I could not make myself completely be in the moment and soak in all that was happening in the present. My mind could not seem to stop thinking about the future and going forward.

Although I wasn't doing much of anything, I could not find rest. Instead of running to God for rest and reassurance, I was running away from Him in an attempt to fill the empty space.

After reading the story of Jesus in the wilderness, I realized that I was experiencing my own wilderness. During this time, the image that I had developed as a little girl changed. There was no sand, dirt, trees, or bushes in my wilderness. The wilderness I was experiencing was figurative, not literal.

When Jesus was in the wilderness, He lacked food and water. In my wilderness, I lacked an immediate answer and a project. At first, I was resentful towards God. I questioned why He would make me go through this difficult time when He could just provide me the answer I desired.

When I finally shifted my attitude from resentment to growth, my entire perspective changed. I stopped viewing my wilderness as a dreadful experience and started to view it as a *necessary* experience. Because I started to stray from God, and my relationship with Him started to weaken, He used a wilderness to bring me back to Him. I eventually used my wilderness to grow. My relationship with Him was strong and alive.

We all go through a wilderness at some point in our lives. We pray for God to rescue us from our struggles and remove the difficult situations. If you are currently struggling to wait for God's answer, or you are in the middle of a difficult time, I encourage you to first identify your desires. What are you yearning for that makes this time of waiting and stillness so difficult? When you declare the things that you strongly desire, you will realize how unnecessary those things are. When I finally identified the things that I desired the most, I discovered that they were wants and not needs. I did not need a project or an answer to be fulfilled. I needed my relationship with Christ to be strong and intimate to fill the empty space.

You might think you need those things that you are waiting on, but what you need more is a relationship with Christ. Sometimes those voids can ONLY be filled with Christ.

I am currently writing this from the recliner in my living room. It is a Saturday night and I am not supposed to leave my house or venture into a public place. The world, and more recently the United States, is experiencing a wilderness.

A rapidly spreading coronavirus, COVID-19, is impacting thousands of people. There is panic, fear, and distress. Everyone is basically stuck inside until further notice.

People all over the world are being deprived of their typical desires. Friends can no longer hang out. Students can not attend school. Non-essential businesses must close. Workers are forced to work from home. Some people lost their jobs. Routines are disrupted.

Although the world appears to be in a state of chaos, stillness is present. I went for a walk today, and as I looked around, I realized how calm everything is. Despite the overall fear and panic that most of the world is experiencing, people are still experiencing peace. I am one of those people. During this break, there are no distractions. I am able to fully focus my attention on Christ. It is through Him that I have found peace during this hectic time.

Matthew 4:1
"Then Jesus was led by the Spirit into the wilderness to be tempted by the devil."

The Holy Spirit led Jesus into a trying time and stayed with Him through a trying time. Jesus' wilderness experience tested Him and His faith. Despite temptation, He did not sin.

I believe that the Holy Spirit led me into my wilderness because I needed my relationship with Christ to grow. I believe that the Holy Spirit was with me the entire time. There were hard times, but the Holy Spirit was always there to redirect me back to Christ.

I also believe that the Holy Spirit did the same thing with the world's current wilderness. Do I believe that God created a disease to kill thousands of people? No. Do I believe that God knew the world needed to come back to Him? Yes. I believe that despite the situation, the Holy Spirit led the world into this wilderness to get people to come back to Him.

Remember when I said that everything seemed calm? That calmness and peace did not just appear out of nowhere. Through this trying time, everyone seems friendly. Everyone is willing to lend a helping hand. People are coming together. The President declared March 15 as National Prayer Day. That says a lot.

Yes, there is sadness, grief, and fear, but there is also peace, hope, and unity. I believe that the Holy Spirit leads us into a wilderness when we need it the most. I believe that the Holy

Spirit is with us every step of the way. I believe that God uses a wilderness, figurative, or literal, to bring us back to Him.

Live in Faith

$\mathcal{Y}$ou have a choice to make every morning when you wake up. You can either live in fear, or you can live in faith.

Fear is sneaky and tricky. There are some days when you feel great, right? Nothing is bothering you, and you're not worried about a single thing. There are some days when it's scary to get out of bed, and you feel like crawling in a hole and not coming out until the day is over.

Fear is hard to overcome because it can be present at the same time as faith. You could be telling yourself that you're fine and that God has it handled, yet in the back of your mind, fear is whispering its crippling words.

How do you get rid of the little voice in the back of your mind for good? How do you choose to live in faith instead of fear? You have to give whatever fear you are holding onto COMPLETELY over to God. Sounds easy, right? But if it were easy, then why are you still hearing that little voice?

Giving everything over to God is hard. I didn't realize how hard it is to make an active choice to live in faith every day until this past year.

For several weeks, I experienced anxiety in social settings. I can't really pinpoint when it started, but it was there. I was always on edge and felt as if someone was always criticizing my every move. My breathing would get heavy and I would start to sweat. It was as if I was waiting for something bad to happen.

Every day, I begged God to take away my anxiety and fear. When I felt anxious, I would say to myself, "You're fine. God's got you." But no matter how many times I declared these words, my anxiety wasn't going away. I still heard that little voice in the back of my mind.

During this time, I was invited to attend Chrysalis, a weekend getaway that my church sponsored. If I'm being transparent and honest, I did not want to go. At all.

In the weeks leading up to the trip, my dread increased. I prayed over and over and over again about having an open mind, but my dread continued to grow. Through it all, I heard God telling me, "You need to go."

The weekend arrived, and thankfully, my friend and sister were also attending the camp. Throughout the entire first day, I kept reminding myself that the trip would soon be over. If this doesn't tell you how much I didn't want to be there, then I don't know what will. During our free time, I even contemplated texting my mom and asking her to come get me.

The first night arrived and I have never experienced something like I experienced that night. We gathered in the chapel and listened to an emotional testimony. After listening to the speaker, we each wrote something that we wanted to give to God on a notecard, and we nailed it to a wooden cross. We retreated to our seats and sat in silence for several minutes.

After what seemed like an eternity, one of the spiritual leaders stood up and announced that if anyone needed to speak to either of them about anything that they were dealing with, they were available. The spiritual leaders each claimed a spot in the sanctuary and waited.

The chapel was completely silent. There were several candles lit, but otherwise, the room was dark. I sat in my chair, twirling my pencil in my hand. *Is anyone going to move? When will this be over?*

Before I realized what was happening, I stood up, and I walked to the front of the chapel. I approached one of the spiritual leaders, and next thing I knew, I was kneeling on the ground in tears. I honestly have no idea how I stood up, let alone walked to the front of the chapel. The spiritual director asked me what was going on, and I choked out, "I have been dealing with anxiety and I don't know what to do." From there, I asked him to pray for me, and he did.

At some point, I started crying. (If you ask my friends, I didn't stop crying the entire trip.) I quickly realized that I was not going to walk away without giving my anxiety completely over to God. My table leader joined me, and she held me as I cried, prayed, and surrendered everything to Him. That night, I found victory in Jesus. I specifically remember telling her, "Wow, I feel physically different. I feel like a new person."

Sometimes life knocks you down. And when it does, you should not get back up. That sounds crazy, right? All the time we hear if you get knocked down, get up and try again. But what if we stayed down for just a little bit longer?

Sometimes it takes falling on our knees...literally...to get back up. It takes kneeling and praying to get the help we truly need. If we get back up too quickly, all we're doing is adding some cheap masking tape to something that's seriously broken. We're not fixing the problem, we're just covering it up. So if you get knocked down, I encourage you to stay down for just a moment longer, long enough to come to God and to be healed. He is our rock, right? The safest place we can be is sitting right on top of Him, relying on His strength, even if that means hitting rock bottom. We get easily confused though. Rock bottom could be disguised as something bad, something totally unappealing. If God is your rock, you're not hitting the bottom. You're hitting strength, love, comfort, peace, and rest. When we hit rock bottom, we're forced to feel that we have nothing else to rely on. It allows us to fully rely on God's strength. Sometimes rock bottom is the safety net that we didn't know we needed.

I felt so loved and safe that night, crying on the chapel floor, that I did not want to get back up because I knew that God was holding me. I knew that God was supporting me with His strength.

My table leader said something to me that night that I will always remember. She told me, "You put it down, now don't pick it back up."

You can pray all you want for God to take your burden away from you, but let me ask you a question: how can He take it if you're still holding onto it? You have to give it to Him and let it go. If you pray for Him to break that chain, He will break it, but it will only stay broken if you let it stay broken. It will only stay broken if you don't allow yourself to pick it back up.

Surrendering whatever burden that you are carrying around to God is hard. Maybe on some level, you have a hard time trusting that He will actually take it. You might have a hard time trusting that you will actually be relieved of that burden.

If you feel this way about whatever you are facing, I know the feeling. Even though I kept saying that God had it handled, I did not fully believe or trust that He would actually take it until that night in the chapel. If you're having a hard time fully giving it to God and letting the chain be broken, stop focusing on the burden for a moment and start focusing on fully trusting Him.

On a lighter note, allow me to share with you a comical story. At one point during the experience, I heard someone let out a loud cry. *Woah, that person is really struggling.* Turns out, that person was my sister, but I'll get to that later. When I say loud cry, I mean LOUD cry. It sounded like someone was in some serious agony.

As I made my way back to our cabin, I could not believe how amazing I felt. I was the first person back, so I jumped in the shower and continued to be amazed by God's amazing grace and goodness. I went to bed that night feeling more peace and love than I have ever felt.

Oh, did I mention that we were not allowed to talk this entire time? The chapel was not the only thing that was silent. From 8:00 that night until 8:00 the next morning, we were silent and in a time of reflection. When we were finally able to speak, my friend, sister, and I met in our cabin at one of the bathroom breaks. As we waited for the break to be over, we discussed the events of the previous night. Somebody mentioned that they could not believe that I was the first person to walk upfront. I responded, "Yeah, I know. I couldn't believe that either. Did you hear the person that let out that loud cry? I hope they're okay."

Instead of saying something, my sister started laughing, and I instantly knew exactly why. Breathless and giggling, she squeaked, "That was me." It took us several minutes to calm down and contain our laughter after that one.

On the first night of the trip, I chose to live in faith. Don't assume that every day since then has been a breeze. I have good days, and I have bad days. On the bad days, I now have confidence that if I give my fears to God, He'll break the chains. I also know that it's up to me to leave them broken.

As I mentioned before, choosing to live in faith is an active, everyday choice. Choosing to live in fear does not just mean asking God to take away your fears. He is not the only one who has a job to do. In order to live in faith, you have to choose to give everything to Him.

Living in faith also means not allowing fear to have ANY control over you. If you allow fear to own your life, then yes, you're going to live in fear. But if you look fear, or whatever you are afraid of, in the eye and tell it about your God, it won't stand a chance.

As I write this, I am listening to "Stand in Your Love." It is such a powerful song because one of the verses says, "Fear doesn't stand a chance when I stand in your love." When we welcome Christ and turn away fear, we are free. We are free of fear and full of faith.

The choice to live in faith does not just present itself in the morning either. Have you heard someone say that you shouldn't go to bed angry? The same thing applies here.

Matthew 6:34 (NIV)
"Therefore Do not worry about tomorrow, for tomorrow will worry about itself. Each day has enough trouble of its own."

Don't go to bed anxious. Don't go to sleep holding onto your fears. If you go to sleep anxious and afraid, you're going to wake up feeling the same way and afraid of the same things. It makes zero sense to live in yesterday's fear because yesterday has already passed. As the verse stated above, the current day that lies ahead of you has enough trouble of its own. Each day, you have a battle to fight. But each day, you have God to walk right beside you and help you fight that battle.

When you feel that fear creep in, don't allow yourself to indulge in those fearful thoughts. You might not have control over the situation, but you have control of your mind. Tell your fears about how great your God is, and let Him do the rest.

Today, I had to make the choice to live in faith multiple times. If I'm being honest with myself, I did not do a great job. My admissions counselor sent me a message that included a Bible verse.

Matthew 28:20 (NIV)
"...and teaching them to obey everything I have commanded you. And surely I am with you always, to the very end of the age."

I read this verse and I was immediately filled with fear. As I type this, I am thinking the exact same thing that you are: shouldn't reading a Bible verse fill you with peace, not fear? I was not even afraid of anything before I read that verse, but I allowed the enemy to use fear to distract me and to control my mind. When I read that verse, I thought, *Is this God's way of warning me about something bad that is going to happen today?* As the day continued to progress, I found myself waiting for something bad to happen. Even though I kept reminding myself that even IF something bad happened that God would be with me, I could not shake the fearful thoughts that flooded my mind. They continued to dwell in my head until I remembered an important lesson that I learned.

Several weeks ago, I stumbled upon an acronym that Jordan Lee Dooley, a New York Times Bestselling author, shared for the word fear:

F. alse
E. vidence
A. bout
R. eality

When you seriously consider the message in that phrase, you eventually realize how silly you're [2]being. Today was one of those days that I had to remind myself to stop being ridiculous. I was allowing "false evidence," or rather no evidence at all, to scare me. After realizing my silly mistake, I re-read the message that my admissions counselor sent me. She was simply sharing an encouraging Bible verse with someone in the middle of a pandemic. (In case you're reading this down the road, or need a reminder, the world is currently battling a deadly coronavirus and is in a state of a pandemic. What a time to write a book, right?)

Discernment helped me to seek peace and to choose to live in faith today. Discernment is not a natural skill. You can not wake up one morning and suddenly be able to distinguish between the enemy's lies and God's truth. It is a skill that must be learned through experience and adapted through the Word.

As I was mindlessly scrolling through Instagram one day, I came across a quote that made me pause:

"One of the biggest red flags that God gives us is the absence of his peace." [3]

---

[2] Jordan Lee Dooley shared this quote through her Instagram page.
[3] Anonymous quote from social media

That quote made me stop and think really hard. One of the most important things that I have learned is that God's peace is significant and telling.

I have officially reached the age where exploring college options is not in the future; it is in the present. On December 4, 2019, my mom, dad, sister, and I visited Lancaster Bible College. I was super excited about the visit because of the proximity to home, small campus, and emphasis on Christ. The night before we visited the campus, I asked God to speak to me. I asked Him to guide me, direct me, and tell me if LBC was the college that I should attend. As soon as we stepped onto the campus, I felt comfortable. We were welcomed with love and greeted with countless smiles.

For the first part of the visit, we got to attend their tri-weekly, mandatory chapel. I'm usually intimidated by people who I don't know, especially people that are slightly older than me. Although the room was filled with strangers, I felt safe. I was not worried about what people would think about me.

At the beginning of the service, the student band led us through worship music. During the second song, I felt an overwhelming sense of peace. By overwhelming, I mean OVERWHELMING. As I write this, I get chills just thinking about it. At that moment, I felt God's peace like I have never felt it before, and I knew that God was directing me down the right path. God spoke to me and answered my prayer.

Over time, I have learned that discernment is a very important skill to learn. When your faith is tested, being able to distinguish between God's voice and the world's voice will be crucial. My faith was tested today, and I'm thankful that I was able to distinguish between the enemy's lies and God's truth.

Will I ever be able to master the art of discernment? Probably not because nobody is perfect. Will I be able to live in faith constantly? No, because I am human and not being afraid of anything is nearly impossible. (I say nearly because NOTHING is impossible with God.) However, applying the Word to my life and relying on God's peace to guide me will not only strengthen my discerning skills but also help me to live in faith.

I encourage you to spend some time in prayer. Ask God to help you be able to distinguish between His voice and the world's voice. Remember, you won't be a master overnight, so give yourself some grace. It's hard to live in faith, but it's also worth it.

Resist, Resist, Resist

I'm writing this while sitting on my bed. If there's one thing that I can assure you of, it is that my bed wears many hats. It provides a place where I can sleep, it serves as my prayer corner, it is the place where many ideas have been cooked up and brought into fruition, and it is my safe place. When I'm happy, I can sit criss-cross-applesauce and cry tears of joy. When I can't sleep, I can talk to my sister and giggle at one of her ridiculous jokes. When I'm feeling upset, I can cry, pray, and seek comfort.

My bed is not the only place where I have found comfort. As I sat on my bed tonight, criss-cross-applesauce to be specific, and read my Bible, I came across several verses that brought my anxious heart the comfort that it needed. My anxiety weighed heavy on my shoulders today, and this scripture was sent straight from God.

> ### 1 Peter 5:7 (NIV)
> **"Cast all your anxiety on him because he cares for you."**

This verse has been a favorite of mine for quite some time. It is such an uplifting reminder that God will not only care for me but that He will also accept my burdens. I do not have to carry my anxiety around. When I re-read this verse tonight, my anxiety did not seem so bad anymore. I could feel God lifting it off of my shoulders.

The remaining verses are verses that I am not familiar with. Although I have never read them or heard them in my life, I am very glad that God led me to them tonight.

---

1 Peter 5:8 (NIV)
"Be alert and of sober mind. Your enemy the devil prowls around like a roaring lion looking for someone to devour."

The verse above compares the enemy to "a roaring lion looking for someone to devour." I could not come up with a better comparison. The enemy is always waiting for you to let your guard down. It is waiting for you to succumb to your weaknesses.

---

1 Peter 5:9 (NIV)
"Resist him, standing firm in the faith, because you know that the family of believers throughout the world is undergoing the same kind of sufferings."

After reading this verse, I wrote in my notes, "resist, resist, resist." I reminded myself that with God, I can resist the enemy. I do not have to succumb. With God, nothing is impossible. Verse 9 is also a very good reminder that you are never alone. Not a single person is strong all the time. We all suffer. We all succumb. We are all weak at some point.

> ## 1 Peter 5:10 (NIV)
> "And the God of all grace, who called you to his eternal glory in Christ, after you have suffered a little while, will himself restore you and make you strong, firm and steadfast."

God is not only ready to wrap His arms around you in comfort, but He is also ready to shower you with grace. You are not expected to be strong and upright all of the time. When you do get knocked down, remind yourself of this truth: God is ready to pick you back up and restore you. He is ready to strengthen you and to help you grow.

What are you battling right now? What weakness is the enemy using against you? Be honest with yourself. We all have that one thing that reminds us that we are weak. For me, anxiety is my daily reminder that I need God. I need Him to provide me strength, peace, and comfort. I need Him to help me resist the enemy, and you need Him too. Find your safe place. Find comfort in Him and His word. Resist, resist, resist.

He's Got You Covered

I have doubted myself countless times over the past couple of years. Thankfully, no matter how many times I doubt myself, God will always be there to reassure me.

I remember when I self-published my first devotional, I was bursting with pride and excitement. The thought that I might be disappointed with the finished copy *never* crossed my mind.

I received an email confirming the delivery date the week before we went on a family vacation to the Outer Banks. I had been anticipating the arrival of the published books for several weeks, so I was very disappointed when I found out that they would be arriving while we were on vacation. After getting over my disappointment, I told myself not to worry about the books. I gave my grandma strict instructions to pick up the delivered package and leave the box completely sealed. I made it very clear to her that I did not want her to look at the books before I did.

Sometime between the email confirmation and the delivery of the books, I had a nightmare that every single copy had several typos. I remember telling my family about the terrible dream that I had, and they all kindly told me that the books would turn out great. (This seems like a good time to tell you that I had NOBODY proofread my work.) You wouldn't expect a dream about typos in a book to be classified as a nightmare, but it was to me.

During our vacation, I could not wait to get home so that I could look at the books. When we finally got home, opening the package was one of the first things that I did. I frantically flipped through the pages to locate any typos. I was convinced that I would find one, and I did.

Turns out, there was more than just that one typo. After my grandma and my mom read the book, they shared with me that one of the Bible verses did not match the one devotional that I wrote. Upon investigation of the mistyped verse, I discovered that they were correct. The Bible verse had absolutely NOTHING to do with the devotional, and that was not even the worst part. I had already distributed several devotionals to close family and friends.

I was very disappointed, so I did the only thing that I thought I could do: use a label maker to individually correct each devotional. It took me forever, and the labels were not subtle. Any person with functioning eyes could tell that there was a label stuck to the middle of the page.

Eventually, I did correct the mistake the "proper" way. When I ordered the next shipment of devotionals, I made sure that I would not have to correct any mistakes with a label maker.

A few weeks ago, I started to edit the devotional. My plan was to revise the entire book and get an updated copy printed. As I started to edit each page with a fine-toothed comb, I found myself disappointed with my work again. Before I realized what was happening, I started changing most of the original writing. Every word seemed to scream, "Fix me!" I got to page six and stopped. *What am I doing?*

I soon realized that my first self-published book was not supposed to be perfect. My first book was a stepping stone. It taught me a VERY important lesson: it's okay to fail.

In school, I have never really been faced with failure. I have always gotten straight A's (except one B in social studies in eighth grade. I might still be bitter about that one). At the time, I viewed the devotional as a failure, and I had a hard time accepting that the book was not perfect.

Despite my doubt and disappointment, there was one person who continued to believe in me: God. He didn't care that I had typos and errors. He cared that I listened to His direction and shared His word with other people. He called me to ministry, and I listened. That's what mattered.

My devotional was not the only time that God had to remind me that His grace will always cover my imperfections and "failures." Every year at my church, we perform the story of Christmas for the congregation on Christmas Eve. This past year, I was the Archangel and I felt completely prepared. At every practice, I knew exactly when to say my lines and when to exit the stage. Although I didn't have my lines fully memorized, I knew the dynamics of the performance.

I wasn't as prepared as I had thought. I left the stage too soon and entirely skipped one of my lines. I also read the rest of the line without my microphone turned on behind the backdrop where no one could see me. For a split second, I was upset with myself, despite the fact that it was a children's Christmas place.

I have always been hard on myself to succeed and to deliver something with grace and flawlessness. Once I got over my initial disappointment, I started to laugh. I had a huge smile on my face because God reminded me that no matter how bad I messed up, it didn't matter. What mattered was His story and sharing it with the rest of the world, even though I skipped a minor part in our annual Christmas program.

I have a tendency to dwell on every mistake I make. If I park crooked in a parking lot, I'll dwell on it for five minutes. I have a rough time forgiving myself for my mistakes and moving on from the situation.

This past July, I hosted a faith night at my church. I had been planning the night for nearly six months and held some pretty high standards for myself. My plan was to speak, sing some worship songs, and fellowship afterward.

When the night finally arrived, that's exactly what happened. I spoke, sang some worship songs with the congregation, and fellowshipped with members afterward. Although the night ran smoothly, I wasn't happy when I went home that night. I felt like a failure, and disappointment weighed on my heart.

I initially attributed my disappointment to not having a plan. Once the night was over, I no longer had a project to work on or something to pour my energy into. The only thing for me to do was to be still and rest. I was miserable, had a bad attitude, and was angry with God for not telling me what to do next.

Looking back, my disappointment was not caused by uncertainty about the future. It was caused by my outrageous expectations. I went into the night expecting the sanctuary to be packed. That expectation is far from the reality of the situation. Around 40 people showed up that night, and half of those people were my family and youth group who were "required" to attend. I should have been happy with that number and glad that my words reached at least one person that night. Instead, I felt like a failure because my outrageous expectations were not met.

This experience taught me to keep my expectations to a minimum. I set myself up for disappointment when I expected the night to be perfect. I'm not saying we shouldn't dream big because anything is possible with God. I'm saying that we should allow room for failure, and prepare ourselves if failure is the outcome. We are not perfect and there will be times when we fail our own expectations and the expectations of others.

That night, my message was far from flawless. There were times where I stumbled over my words, spoke too quickly, or didn't quite think it through ahead of time.

Instead of wallowing in my disappointment, I should have been praising God for loving and blessing me despite my failures. Even though my faith night was littered with imperfections, God still loved me, was still there for me, and he did not abandon me. His grace covered my mistakes.

The next time you're planning something, remind yourself that God does not expect us to be perfect. He welcomes our failure instead of rejecting it. Give yourself some grace and allow some room for failure. Above all else, believe that you are covered by God's grace. I am thankful that I experienced failure and disappointment because it taught me that failure is vital for growth.

Difficult and uncomfortable situations are also vital for growth. Everyone has that one job or chore that they hate, absolutely despise. When our parents or a peer asks us to do that job or chore, we complain, right? When my dad asks me to pick up sticks at our piece of land, I usually come up with a lousy excuse to get out of it. (For the record, I have NEVER picked up the sticks.)

There have been numerous occasions where God has taken on the role of my parents or peers. He asks me to do something, and I respond with a complaint. *Why me God? Why can't You just handle it or assign it to someone else?* Easy, enjoyable tasks are comforting. Hard, uncomfortable tasks make us feel really uneasy.

This past school year, God gave me a really hard task. I have a fellow classmate that works on my nerves. I know that sounds very blunt and direct, but it is the truth. We do not have the same values or morals. We do not hang out with the same crowds. We do not have hardly anything in common. To prove my point even farther, this particular classmate usually picks on me. At school, I tend to be very reserved. I refrain from leaving my little comfortable bubble.

One day, during history class, my teacher decided to switch up the seating chart. As you probably have already assumed, the teacher sat this particular student right in front of me. For the most part, I tolerated the situation. I did not start up a conversation unless they spoke to me first. It was easier for me to pretend that they were not even there.

The pretending got really hard, really fast when this person called me out in front of everyone during a class discussion.

Anyone who knows me can agree that I do not dance. If you ask my sister, I have zero rhythm and coordination when it comes to dancing to music. At school dances, I usually just stand around my friends while they dance to whatever music the DJ decides to play.

The discussion in class shifted to the topic of the homecoming dance. I do not remember how, or why, but my teacher looked at me and asked me if I dance at the school dances. I simply shook my head no. While I was replying to the teacher, the student in front of me started chuckling. Unfortunately, the teacher questioned the student and asked, "Oh, is that not true? Does Dylin dance?"

I do not remember exactly how they worded it, but they made it a point to respond that I dance inappropriately. To make matters worse, I blush very easily. So of course, in typical Dylin-fashion, I turned bright red. The student to my right made sure to point out the fact that I was blushing as if it was not abundantly obvious. The entire class laughed and stared at me. I fought back tears, and I do not remember a single thing that we talked about during the rest of the class. I was completely focused on trying not to cry and show everyone how bothered I really was.

I somehow managed to hold back the tears until my way home from school. My closest friend and sister were in the car with me when I finally broke down. My friend just casually brought up the incident in conversation. She was not making fun of me. She was standing up for me and saying that what the student did was rude.

I realize now that I had been letting every word that this student said to me tear me down for weeks. I just refused to acknowledge how much their words actually hurt me. Instead of addressing the problem, I just tried to play it off that I was totally okay with letting them bother me.

I had been praying for this person for quite some time, but I really struggled to pray for my fellow classmate that night. After what they had done, not a single part of me wanted to be kind to them. I told God exactly that, and I expected Him to respond with a comforting word, not a difficult assignment. He told me to not only continue to pray for that person but to talk to them about what had happened. *What? Are You kidding me? How am I even supposed to approach them? How am I going to talk to them without crying again?*

Despite my initial shock and disbelief, a plan started to form in my mind. The logistics of talking to that person were not the problem in forming a plan. It was my unwillingness to trust God and perform the task.

I eventually talked to that person face to face. The next day at school, I tapped them on the shoulder as we were leaving class. I can still picture the shock on their face as they turned around and realized that I was actually confronting them. I told them exactly what bothered me about the situation. Surprisingly, I felt ten times better. I was able to pray for them again, and I was eventually able to forgive them.

I learned an important lesson that day. It is better to talk to someone face to face and layout all your feelings and thoughts than it is to hold onto anger, bitterness, and hurt.

Romans 5:3-4 (NIV)
"Not only so, but we also glory in our sufferings, because we know that suffering produces perseverance; perseverance, character; and character, hope."

You do not grow in comfortable situations. God sometimes assigns us hard tasks because He wants us to grow. In the moment, all we can think about is how much we do not want to do what He is asking us to do. It seems that God is asking us to do something hard out of punishment when in reality He is doing it out of love. is. He wants to challenge us so that we can grow and become a better version of ourselves. Hard tasks are exactly what they are:

hard. They are also rewarding and an incredible opportunity to not only grow as a person, but they also allow us to grow our faith.

My grandparents enjoyed a picnic in my backyard alongside the rest of my family last night. We had previously asked them to join us on a vacation to the Outer Banks. My grandpa made the comment to my dad that he would not be interested, but my grandma might want to tag along. Obviously, we would not turn one or both of them away. They will always be welcome.

At dinner, we brought up the topic again to see what direction they were leaning. My grandpa again said that he did not want to go, but that my grandma did.

My grandma's response stuck with me, and I'm not totally sure why if I'm being honest. She replied, "If we go, we are going together." I thought about her response a lot from the moment it left her mouth until now. Even though my grandma had an opportunity to enjoy something that SHE was interested in doing, she refused to do it without her husband.

Over the course of my life, I have been fortunate to witness unconditional love displayed right in front of me. When my Mimi leaves for a weekend away, she always calls my pa to check in on him. When she leaves their house, or returns, she greets him and says good-bye with a kiss...always.

Her response at the picnic reminded me that love is unconditional. She had to sacrifice a memorable vacation for my grandpa.

Her response, and their relationship as a whole, reminded me of my own relationship with Christ. My grandparents have chosen, and continue to choose to always stick together. I have found that when I always stay close to Christ, not only is my relationship with Him strong, but things are just overall better. I rarely feel as if things will fall apart, and if they do, I know that I have someone standing right beside me to support me.

My Mimi's response also reminded me that having a relationship with Christ will require you to give up something at some point. However, giving something up for a relationship with Him will always result in gaining something better. Because my grandparents make sacrifices and unconditional decisions for each other, their relationship remains strong and intact. Although they have to give something up, they gain a strong relationship in return. When my relationship with Christ became a priority in my life, I also had to make several sacrifices.

Do I consider myself popular? Absolutely not. Am I okay with that? Totally.

In elementary and middle school, you could say that I was a part of the "cool" crowd. You know the group of people that everyone knows and everyone wants to be a part of. There were many people that I considered my friends.

I find it fascinating that my definition of a friend has evolved over time. The people that I use to consider my friends no longer fit my definition. By the time I reached high school, I lost many of those "friends."

I did not just lose them; I chose to give them up. The friends that I chose to keep around were the ones who mattered. They encouraged my relationship with Christ, and they supported my beliefs and morals. They are more than just my friends; they are my community. Does it sadden me to look around at school and not even be able to recognize some people that I once knew? A little bit, yes. Although, I'm quickly reminded that I gained something far better in return.

Growing up, I believed in God. I attended church regularly, and I said my prayers every night. Sunday mornings were always reserved for church. My family always prayed before every meal. I did these things because I didn't know any different. Until about two years ago, I believed in God because my parents believed in God and I was raised in the church.

When you reach high school, you start to make decisions for yourself. Some of my friends who used to attend church, no longer attended. Their Sunday mornings were spent in bed while mine was spent at church. Thankfully, my parents never gave me the option of sleeping in on a Sunday. It was an unspoken rule that the whole family would go to church on a Sunday morning. The foundation they laid for me when I was younger is a large part of who I am today.

About two years ago, my faith and relationship with Christ started to become my own. I no longer believed in God just because my parents believed in Him. I believed in God because I had formed a personal relationship with Him. I began to see for myself who He was, is, and will always be.

The why behind what I believed in started to change when I realized how much I needed God in my life. As I mentioned before, decisions regarding my life started to become my own, not my parents'. There were times when I needed His guidance to make pretty big decisions. On one occasion, God's guidance was different than my parents' advice.

I was sitting in study hall one day, and the guidance counselor called me into her office. Because I rarely get called to the office, I was a little bit concerned. *Am I in some sort of trouble?* When I reached the guidance counselor's office, she told me to have a seat. *Okay, what's going on?* She proceeded to tell me that I was selected to attend a leadership conference at Messiah College. I was instantly excited. At the time, Messiah College was a school that I was interested in attending. It would be an amazing opportunity to meet people, learn some leadership skills, and visit a school that I was interested in.

After leaving her office, I visited my mom's office to tell her the exciting news. As I started to tell my mom the details about the conference, I noticed that the expression on her face changed. She reached in her drawer and pulled out her pocketbook calendar. (Yes, she's behind the times and refuses to use the calendar on her phone.) She quickly flipped through the pages and said, "Uh, oh. The conference is the same week as the mission trip." My excitement about the conference instantly vanished. I had been looking forward to this mission trip for months.

That night at dinner, we told my dad about the opportunity and discussed our options. Basically, I had to choose between the mission trip and the leadership conference. Looking back, this was probably the first big decision that I faced.

As I stepped into the shower that night, I cried simply because I did not know what to do. My parents were letting the decision in my hands, and at the moment it felt as if God was doing the same. After praying and asking God for guidance, I quickly realized that God was actually leading me towards the mission trip. I felt peace and the decision went from difficult to extremely clear.

To some of you, this decision might not seem that big. But to a 16-year-old, it was a big deal.

It was also a very defining moment in my life. Sometimes it takes a difficult situation to realize the role that God actually plays in your life. It made me realize that I need God. I need Him to help me make tough decisions, to hold me accountable, and to keep me on track. I need Him to simply be there with me every minute of every day.

Before the trip began, I was afraid that I had lost an incredible opportunity that I might never be able to experience again. I can confidently say that I did not lose anything. Instead, I gained a stronger relationship with Christ, new friends, and incredible experiences.

I want to tell you about a particular experience that I will never forget. For a few days, my group was assigned to work on a man's house that was completely destroyed by flooding. We had to clean out the damaged items and prepare the house for construction and renovation. As we began to tackle the project, we quickly realized that almost everything was damaged. We spread a giant tarp on the grass in front of the house and started to gather the items that could potentially be salvaged.

Every day the man would sit in a chair in the shade and watch us work. Although he left the property frequently, he always came back to sit in the same spot. There were several times where some of us would gather around him and simply fellowship with him. I can't even imagine the thoughts that ran through the man's head as he watched what little possessions he had left be thrown onto a tarp in his front yard.

On our last day at the man's house, I approached him and offered him one of the devotional books that I wrote. He accepted the book graciously and carried the book into his gutted house.

Later that day, I entered through the back door of the house and looked around the small kitchen. After previously emptying the space, all that remained was a kitchen table and a refrigerator. As I scanned the area and soaked in the progress that we had made, my eyes landed on a specific item on the table. The table was littered with some food items and miscellaneous papers. There was a microwave and maybe a few cans of soup. Laying amongst the items was my devotional. It touched my heart to know that one of the man's few possessions was my book. He gave that little 50-page book, filled with errors, a spot on his broken kitchen table that resided in his empty house.

I would not have gained the most humbling experience of my life if my decision regarding the trip was different. A relationship with Christ will require us to give up something that seems important to us. It will also allow us to gain something better than we could ever imagine.

Psalm 63

I was not planning on including this chapter. I was not even planning on writing it. But hey, if this year has taught me anything, it's that plans change. A lot.

Several days ago, I made a promise to myself to dive into God's word more than I had previously been doing. You might think that I read my Bible diligently. If I'm being honest, it's one of my biggest weaknesses. Most of my Bible reading comes from the daily verse notification I get on my phone and the single verse that is included in my daily devotional. I decided that I needed to seriously improve this area of my life, so I made a change. I told myself that every night I was going to spend some quality, focused time reading a passage of the Bible.

Tonight, as I read my selected passage, I was seriously inspired. I want to note that I randomly selected Psalm 63. I literally opened my Bible, and I fanned the pages until I landed on a random passage.

What do you think the odds are that I would land on a chapter that basically outlined every thought and realization that I have had over the past two years? If you are trying to come up with a percentage or some statistic, please stop because there are no odds. There is God.

Take a moment and read Psalm 63. As I read this passage, I started taking notes in the margins. I started reflecting on how much this passage meant to me. I quickly realized that the meaning that Psalm 63 has to me belonged in this book.

My favorite verse in the whole chapter is the very first one.

Psalm 63:1 (NIV)
"You, God, are my God, earnestly I seek you; I thirst for you, my whole being longs for you, in a dry and parched land where there is no water."

There have been times where I was definitely lacking water. I was parched and dry. Yet no matter what I tried to quench this thirst with, I still felt parched. God has shown me that there is nothing that can replace Him. We run to so many things trying to fill a void that can not be filled with anything but God. If you're feeling parched, stop drinking the world and start drinking God. Fill your life with Him, read His Word, and talk to Him.

Psalm 63:3 (NIV)
"Because your love is better than life, my lips will glorify you."

The third verse also struck me. When is the last time you have taken a moment to simply soak in God's love? To remember the magnitude of it? God's love for us is bigger than anything on this earth, and for that reason, we need to use our lives to glorify Him. God called me to minister to others through my voice, whether that be verbally or written. There are times where I do not want to. I am not the biggest fan of having all of the attention on me.

In fact, I'm uncomfortable when everyone in a room is looking at me. When I have these thoughts, I force myself to be reminded of what Jesus did for us. He gave up His life for us. If He could die a brutal death on the cross for me, then I can endure a few moments of uncomfortableness for Him. We don't grow when we're comfortable. We grow when our faith is tested and we're put in an uncomfortable situation.

I did not just get through those uncomfortable situations by reminding myself. I got through them because I clung to God's strength.

Psalm 63:8 (NIV)
"I cling to you; your right hand upholds me."

People often say that the strongest people are the ones who ask for help when they need it. I am definitely guilty of needing help and not asking for any. However, I've learned that God will never decline my request. If you need help, ask for it. If you need strength, reach out to Him. He will keep you upright and provide exactly what you need. Compared to Him, we are so weak. There will be times when our strength is not enough. Thankfully, God's strength will ALWAYS be enough.

If you have gained nothing else from these pages highlighting Psalm 63, then learn this: read your Bible. You never know what God will choose to share with you.

Age Is Just a Number

Do you remember when you were little and your dad would say to you, "You throw like a girl?" Maybe you do, maybe you don't. In my experience, the phrase hardly ever comes from a place of positivity.

Because I never made it past T-ball when I was little, the phrase was never really said to me, but I can relate to the people who have had this phrase directed at them in another way.

When my aunts or uncles or relatives would come to my soccer games when I was little, they would always call me prancer. Because I also took dance class at the time, I did not run super athletically. My family members said that I pranced across the field. Picture a baby deer running across a soccer field. That was me.

When they called me this, it honestly didn't feel great. I might have only been 8 years old, but it wasn't like they were complimenting me. In a roundabout way, they were expressing that I did not live up to their standards of how a soccer player should run. They might not have meant that, but that is exactly how I interpreted it. It felt as if they were saying, "You throw like a girl," but in an entirely different situation and in an entirely different way.

I encountered a similar experience when I shared a message at my church during our Sunday service last fall. After the service, several of my family members approached me and said, "Good job, Dylin." In your opinion, this probably seems like the perfect thing to say to someone after they get done speaking or accomplishing something.

Instead, it actually felt like they were saying, "That was a great message...for a 16-year-old." Unless you have been in my shoes or experienced something similar, you probably think that I'm either crazy, ungrateful or just reading more into their words than what they actually meant.

Let me ask you something though. Have you ever walked up to the pastor at your church, or a speaker at an event in general, and said, "Good job"? Or have you said, "Wow, that was such a great message"?

I'm not sharing this experience with you or asking you these questions to make you feel guilty and bad about yourself. I'm also not sharing them because I want you to stop complimenting people and telling them that they did a great job. I just want to share what I have felt over the past couple of years.

As I mentioned before, I have doubted myself a lot. I'm doubting myself while typing this on my Chromebook, in my living room, as my dad watches Wicked Tuna. I have asked, and continue to ask, myself a lot of questions, questions that are not always confidence-boosting. *Am I really qualified for this? Am I too young to be leading others? Will people relate to the things that I'm writing or speaking about? Will they take them seriously? Is this book too short?*

Whenever people would tell me "Good job," their words only seemed to fuel the doubts that I already had about myself. (My logic or feelings still probably don't make any sense in your head. Just hear me out.)

Tonight at my youth group, I taught the lesson. In the past, I was never able to feel joy after sharing a message, and I was never able to understand why. I would always ask myself the questions above and replay everything that went wrong in my head.

Tonight was an entirely different story. After I shared my message, my sister looked at me and said, "That was a really good message." She probably did not even realize how much her words impacted me. Although my youth leader messaged me afterward and said "Great job," I read her words exactly how she meant that: that I had done a great job sharing the message.

I cried tears of joy and gratitude tonight when I prayed because I was finally able to accept their words for what they were. I didn't read into them at all. I was finally able to feel joy after sharing a message.

In the past, I never allowed myself to accept someone's compliment or kind words because I convinced myself that they were only saying those things because they were "supposed" to say them. I always felt that they were only complimenting me because I had failed to live up to their standards and that they wanted to be polite.

Tonight, my sister said something else that assured me that she truly meant it when she said, "That was a really good message."Roughly thirty minutes after our youth group ended, I doubtfully asked her, "Are you sure my lesson was good."

She simply replied, "Yes, it was good. I would tell you if it wasn't." That right there is the response of a true friend who not only loves you but keeps you accountable.

Do you ever feel like you're fighting a losing battle when it comes to keeping up with someone else's standards? No matter how well you do something, there will always be something wrong with what you did in their eyes. I recently read on social media that even if you are the world's best and juiciest peach, there will always be someone who doesn't like peaches.

As I told God how grateful I was tonight, a Bible verse came to my mind:

> ## 1 Timothy 4:12 (NIV)
> **"Don't let anyone look down on you because you are young, but set an example for the believers in speech, in conduct, in love, in faith, and in purity."**

My youth group has used this verse as our motto because it reminds us that although we are young, we still have a purpose. We are still called to serve others and share God's love with the world.

Tonight this verse reminded me that I am not too young. I am not unqualified. If God places a message on my heart and prompts me to share it with the people around me, I am capable. Age does not matter when it comes to fulfilling your God-given purpose. You could be 5, telling your friends that Jesus loves you. You could be 28, inviting your co-worker to church with you on a Sunday morning. You could be 90, barely able to walk without assistance, and still, be capable of sharing God's love with the rest of the world.

My great-grandma Paul reminds me of the 90-year old that I just described. When she was 90, she still played the piano. I remember a specific time that we went to visit her at the assisted living facility where she resided. She sat down at the piano and began to play Amazing Grace. Even though her youth had dwindled away, she did not stop praising God. She was one of the most faithful women that have been a part of my life. Although she's hanging out with Jesus in Heaven, she still inspires me to share my faith with the rest of the world. I often think about her when I stumble across a certain passage in the Bible, or when I hear a certain song.

My point is, your age is just a number. The world requires you to have so many things before you can be deemed successful, or "qualified." A degree, job experience, and certain traits are all a part of what goes into determining the world's standards.

Do you know what God requires? None of that. He just asks that you be willing to say yes. He asks that You step out in faith and confidence. He can, and will, use you. It doesn't matter who you are.

You're never going to be a peach that everyone wants to eat. When you stop living for the world's standards, and you start being confident in your God-given purpose, you will not feel exhausted. You will not feel like you are fighting a losing battle that will never end.

I encourage you to keep stepping out in faith, to keep serving others, and to keep sharing God's love with the world because you might be the only Bible that someone reads someday. You might be the reason that someone comes to know Christ.

For several years, I have tried to convince my friend to come to youth group with me. Repeatedly, she has turned me down. I reached a point where I finally said, "God, I tried. I don't know what else to do." He simply responded that all I needed to do was be an example and let Him do the rest. It filled me with joy when she reached out to me several months ago sharing that she purchased a new Bible. Sometimes, you simply need to plant a seed in someone's life and show them how amazing a relationship with God truly is.

I don't know about you, but when I see Him face to face, I want Him to look at me and say, "Well done my good and faithful servant, well done." Until that day comes, I will not stop fulfilling my God-given purpose. I will not stop responding to His mission, the same mission that He gave you:

> ### Matthew 28:19-20 (NIV)
> **"Therefore go and make disciples of all nations, baptizing them in the name of the Father and of the Son and of the Holy Spirit, and teaching them to obey everything I have commanded you. And surely I am with you always, to the very end of the age."**

I could try to encourage you further, but instead, I would rather leave you with this question:

What do you want God to say to you when you see Him face to face?

I Believe

A few nights ago I read a devotional that really made me question myself. The topic was sharing your faith.

If someone asked y[4]ou right now what your faith means to you, what would you say?

It took me a few minutes to decide what my answer would be. The devotional also reminded me of a time when someone asked me a similar question. At my youth group and church, we talk about what we would say if someone questioned us about our faith and Christ. I could never relate to anyone when we talked about this topic because no one had ever asked me.

A few months ago, I finally experienced one of these situations. My high school put on the musical "Godspell" this past year, and my math partner was a member of the cast. We were sitting in Trigonometry, and she asked me if I would come watch the production. Because I did not know what the musical was

---

[4] Live in Light: 5-minute devotions for teen girls

Melanie Redd

Emeryville, California

2019

Althea Press

Pg. 76

about, I asked her. Instead of answering my question, my partner responded, "Would you consider yourself a religious person?"

Did she really just ask me this question in the middle of math class? I thought about my response for several seconds, and I realized that I would not be able to avoid answering her question. I replied, "No, I don't think I would. My faith is my life, and it is more than just a religion. It is a relationship with God." I was initially afraid that she would judge me for my response, but she didn't. She simply said, "Okay, you should come to the musical."

As I relived this day a few nights ago, I realized that if someone were to ask me this question right now, I would simply hand them this book. I would not have been able to answer this question two years ago, but now I can confidently say that I believe in Him. I have learned that claiming that you are a Christian is pointless without believing who Christ is and what He did for you with your whole heart.

Hebrews 11:6 (NIV)
"And without faith, it is impossible to please God, because anyone who comes to him must believe that he exists and that he rewards those who earnestly seek him"

In order to find that goodness, you not only need to believe that you will find it, but you also need to believe in the One in which it will flow from. God is good, and we must seek Him to find that goodness. Our circumstances do not determine the goodness that we see on a daily basis. Even if our situation does not present goodness, we will find light if we seek God DURING our circumstances.

What do you believe in? I believe that He sent His one and only Son to this earth in the form of a baby to die and rise again so that I can live eternally. I believe that He won every victory and that He overcame the world. I believe that He will never leave my side and that He will always guide me. I believe that one day I will see Him again in Heaven and that He has a place prepared for me.

God has written a beautiful, yet broken, story for me. He has written one for you, and I want you to be able to see the goodness that lies in every chapter. I want you to be able share your faith and story with the world. Now it is my turn to ask you the question:

What do you believe in, and why?